Selected Pathways to God:
The Intellectual, Psychic, and Spiritual

Colliston R. Rose, MD

authorHOUSE®

AuthorHouse™ LLC
1663 Liberty Drive
Bloomington, IN 47403
www.authorhouse.com
Phone: 1-800-839-8640

Published by AuthorHouse   10/11/2013

ISBN: 978-1-4817-2805-8 (sc)
ISBN: 978-1-4817-2804-1 (e)

Library of Congress Control Number: 2013904475

This book is printed on acid-free paper.

List of Publications

Fundamental Approaches in Mastering the Sciences: A Comprehensive Guide for Students. C. H. Fairfax Co., Baltimore, MD., 1991.

A Method of Mass Cultivation of Sessile Peritrich Protozoa. Trans. Amer. Micros. Soc. 95:541-544, 1976 (with H. E. Finley, Ph.D.).

Harold Eugene Finley: American Negro zoologist and educator (A preliminary biographical and bibliographical sketch). Trans Amer. Micros. Soc. 95:285-296, 1976 (with I. P. Finley).

Dedication

To my parents, Frank B. Rose and Eileen A. Rose, both deceased, as well as siblings Mervyn, June, Junette, Everest, Oswin, Oswald (deceased), Stokeley, and Enric as well as my wife, Joan.

Also, to the Mahanta, the Living ECK Master, Spiritual Masters, and all spiritual teachers and students everywhere.

Table of Contents

Preface

The discussion that follows involves the unusual. A proper understanding of what follows is dependent on the ability to think in the non-traditional manner, that is, literally outside the box.

From a recent review of the literature, it is clear that seeking an education, then employment, raising a family if desired and pursuing rest and relaxation are all secondary to working with the Creator as a Co-worker in an increasingly responsible manner.

For many persons, life begins in the cradle and ends at the grave. However, evidence is mounting that one survives death not in the physical form but in the spiritual. We are Soul, a spark or particle of God. Soul is immortal. Furthermore, for us, the human body is the temporary residence of Soul while on earth, and from which it departs and returns during sleep, or leaves permanently at death. Soul's quest is to be a Co-worker with God, and eventually, to return to its kingdoms, its true home.

God lives on floor twelve of a spiritual mansion, literally; by comparison, the earth is floor one. Therefore, Soul seeks a two-, or three-pronged education on earth, and elsewhere, to find a job, pay a rent, raise a family if desired, and find ways to return to its true home. In so doing, it must convert its immaturity to maturity, and spiritual infancy to mastership.

Two well-known training pathways exist for taking Soul into God's kingdoms while still living. These are the Intellectual, favored by science and others, that uses the five physical, or objective, senses and the Psychic (such as old-age and modern religions, yoga, mysticism, and others) that employs the five spiritual, or subjective, senses. Since 1965, however, a third major pathway that existed since time immemorial but which was either hidden, or cryptic, emerged. This is Advanced religion (Eckankar) or Spirituality, that also employs the subjective senses. These three pathways can be rank-ordered and relate to how far into God's kingdoms one can reach. Moreover, two mechanisms are employed when exploring the kingdoms of God. First is the mind that has limitations; then the second mechanism, Soul, takes over. One's approach to God depends on one's understanding of God.

The text introduces the pathways mentioned, use of two very distinct mechanisms (the mind and Soul) for gleaning information about God, karma and reincarnation that allow one to visit past mistakes for corrective action, as well as the vital need to convert faith and belief into knowledge by means of experimentation.

In old-age and modern religions for the congregation, for example, there is very little, if any, experimentation beyond singing, dancing, praying, fasting, and feasting, and even these are not structured for the collection and analysis of data. In trance-like experiments, the experimentee is not conscious of what transpires.

Other psychic pathways, and the Spiritual pathway, on the other hand, feature profound experimentation for new and advanced students.

Experimentation increases one's awareness (consciousness) considerably while awake as well as when asleep. A German scientist, Kekule, while examining materials in Organic Chemistry and unable to resolve conflicting data fell asleep before his fireplace.

He thus turned off his objective consciousness and turned on his subjective. Thereupon, he dreamt of a snake biting its own tail. Thus, Benzene, an important cyclic compound of tremendous biological importance, was discovered.

Yet, scientists did not key in to the use of subjective techniques in obtaining scientific information due to the lack of techniques.

Experimentation can enhance the development of subjective techniques such as chakra awakening, intuition, exteriorization of consciousness, dream travel, Soul travel, and so on.

Additional discussion examines the mind passions that can preclude spiritual development. These are represented by the acronym, vagal – vanity, anger, greed, attachment to material possessions, and lust. This story of life itself features a Living Master and the devil as teachers and educators.

Many persons pursue a career by investing tremendously in time, effort, and treasure, but after a few years desire a career change. Depending on age, and other factors, this might not be possible or can involve great difficulty.

A similar type of situation occurs when someone pursuing a pathway to God wishes a pathway change. Social and family pressures and absence of clear-cut data on available options may present obstacles for such a person. The text is informative in such matters. In addition, the text intersects religion, science, and healing.

The purpose of this book is not to proselytize but to share recently available information on pathways to God's kingdoms as well as how to get there. Furthermore, here is not an attempt to make the case for the belief that "my God is better than your God;" instead, it is to present recently available options for seeking God.

The focus of this book is an elementary understanding of God and His kingdoms that is not detail-oriented. The reader will have to consult with the various appropriate organizations and programs that can provide this information, whether they be intellectual, psychic, or spiritual. Each of the three programs above has elementary, intermediate, and advanced components.

Finally, the contents of this book represent a wake-up call to action to personally investigate one's spiritual heritage and relationship to the Creator. However, the writer is fully aware that the selection of a pathway to God, at the appropriate time, is the reader's choice. In addition, one will find that one's approach to God will depend on one's understanding of God.

Acknowledgement

This book gives my own spiritual understanding and does not speak for any spiritual path, teacher, or religion. In this book I have made occasional use of certain terms (Eckankar, Eck, Mahanta, and Soul Travel) that are trademarks of Eckankar. This does not imply any endorsement or sponsorship of Eckankar. I have intended only to make a fair use of such terms, recognizing that the rights to their trademark usage belong entirely to Eckankar (www.Eckankar.org).

Many thanks are due Eckankar for permission to use the following copyrighted materials: the four types of karma and the Wheel of the Eighty Four, by Paul Twitchell in the 1972 book, the "Eck-Vidya: Ancient Science of Prophecy," pages 45-46, and 17-18, respectively; and a listing of twelve major religions by Paul Twitchell in the "Spiritual Notebook."

I wish to thank, also, Adherents.com.html for the listing of 22 major religions ranked by size seen in the 2005 article (see the Literature Cited).

Special thanks are due Quest books for the use of a list of 7 chakras seen in the book, "The Chakras," by C. W. Leadbeater, page 7 copyright 1997, the eleventh printing, 2012. This material was reproduced by permission of Quest books, the imprint of the Theosophical Publishing House (www.questbooks.net).

Last, but not least, appreciation is due Dr. Shirley Whiteman for provision of technical computer assistance, as well as Ms. Teri Watkins, Design Consultant, and Mr. John Cain, Email Marketing, at AuthorHouse.

1

Thinking Outside the Box

Some believe that life begins in the cradle and ends at the grave. Therefore, for such individuals, no great preparation is required for an afterlife since, for them, there is none. Such persons often have a mindset that prevents further discussion of this matter and are unwilling to examine any new information on God.

It is a fact of life that some individuals are just not ready to receive or even examine advanced information on God and His kingdoms. Some say that God is neither masculine nor feminine.

For various reasons, such individuals are simply content with their present status in life regarding God. For these individuals, this new information involves too much heavy lifting, too much of an intellectual burden to bear. It is ironic, however, that such persons only seek God when something dramatic occurs, such as loss of a loved one, a sudden illness, or a near-death experience.

The question arises – How can one say something of a spiritual nature to someone without upsetting their innermost sensitivities?

However, for those who see life as continuous beyond death, then they may be aware that some kind of preparation may be required for this new adventure when the time will be due.

Furthermore, for these persons, an array of questions can now be asked, such as, "Where does one go after death?," "How is life over there?," "Are there many steps to take in one's spiritual evolution?," or, "Can one prepare for this journey now?" After examining recently available revelations regarding God and His kingdoms, this new adventure can actually begin now while one is still alive.

According to information that is available today, there is one God; all other identified Gods are either sub-Gods, assistants to God, or messengers of God. Some get this classification confused.

From all available information, it appears that God has many heads of departments to run His kingdoms. If one were to state that one met recently God's right-hand man for Soul Affairs, as have thousands of other individuals, this statement would generate various reactions from awesome to cool, anger to disbelief, derision to hostility, depending on the intellectual, psychic, or spiritual development of the individual responding. More will be said regarding these three types of potential educational pathways. But the previous statement above is the truth that was made possible by revelations in the literature that occurred recently. This individual can inform one of one's past lives as well as the present life.

Furthermore, although all individuals are created equal, there are personal variations in intellectual, psychic, and spiritual development. This is a fact of life.

Training in intellectualism, psychic matters, as well as spirituality, in that order, takes one to increasingly higher levels of understanding and experiences, from fringe to full, that an individual not receiving this training may not believe or even consider possible until this person has received a similar level of instruction.

Therefore, the interpretation of the statement above regarding God's right-hand man for Soul Affairs will vary depending on one's intellectual, psychic, or spiritual status.

It appears that from earliest times to the present, individual mankind has taken evolutionary small steps in intellectual, psychic, and spiritual development, but not at the same pace. In addition, although humans are at the top of the evolutionary ladder in terms of movement to God, spiritually, not all humans are alike, sub-classifications of these individuals are evident.

From the lowest to the highest in spiritual development are: humans with animal-like tendencies, such as rapists and murderers, non-intellectual types for various reasons who can be a danger to themselves and to others due to ignorance, intellectual types of varying degrees, those with psychic abilities, and finally, humans possessing spiritual qualities.

Each of the categories listed above can be further subdivided. Refer to the text for these subdivisions.

A large majority of humanity thinks within a box. Society today largely defines the contours of this box. Science, on the other hand, focuses on a box within the larger box relative to the greater society.

In the discussion that follows, an attempt will be made to either expand the borders of the larger box or to dissolve its borders entirely.

This will involve taking a new look at old information or adding to this information. When thinking outside the box, the unusual replaces the usual.

Nineteen sixty five was a pivotal year in matters relating to God and one's spiritual development since the three major pathways to God mentioned above surfaced publicly, although they existed in the past but were very difficult to discern. These are the Intellectual, the Psychic, and the Spiritual.

The Intellectual pathway largely prepares one for life on earth; whereas, the Psychic and Spiritual pathways largely prepare one for life after death of the physical body, although these can be pursued while one is still alive. The three pathways, in the order presented, represent increasing levels of training, and experiences.

Furthermore, each of these pathways has three different sub-levels, namely, the elementary, the intermediate, and the advanced. This meant that before 1965, those persons choosing a pathway to God, or had one chosen for them, involved themselves lacking all of the information on pathways that is available today.

Although it is one's right to choose a pathway to God that fulfils one's needs, this should be done after all possible information on pathways is examined, not before. However, this is not always possible since, as said earlier, before 1965, information on routes to God were often hidden, or cryptic.

Nineteen sixty five was also important since, as said before, one now had access to two major mechanisms for reaching God's kingdoms, namely, the mind and Soul. The Intellectual and Psychic pathways, respectively, through use of the mind, have the potential to take one one-sixth and almost half-way into God's kingdoms.

On the other hand, by employment of mechanisms of the mind, then Soul, the Spiritual pathway potentially can take one all the way into God's kingdoms. More will be said about this later.

Furthermore, in the Intellectual and Psychic pathways, and even in the initial steps of the Spiritual pathway, when awake the mind tries to suppress information from Soul. However, when asleep, Soul takes control; but on awakening, Soul's messages to the mind are either garbled, lost, or partially, or totally recalled, all depending on the stage of one's psychic or spiritual development.

In the absence of clear-cut spiritual guidance, from infancy to adulthood, one is like a puppet on a string. In the background and unknown to most of us, some unknown benevolent force tries to guide us, to groom us, as well as protect us until we can take care of ourselves spiritually. Do such forces or beings really exist? Why help us in the first place? Do we listen to or react to these inner nudges? If we do, we may find that life is like a distance race. Instead of a race for a single lifetime, it is one for multiple lifetimes. Only the brave, fearless, benevolent, loving of all life, and knowledgeable will reach the finish line.

Furthermore, did you ever find yourself in the right place and at the right time that promoted a greater understanding of God?

Many persons do not realize that various pathways to God exist beside old-age and modern religions. It is unfortunate, however, that the reaction to any new information regarding God varies understandably from lack of interest to fervent denial, from disbelief to tacit acceptance of it, from eagerness to examine this information immediately to scrutiny in a cautious, more leisurely manner.

2

Echoes from the Past

Until very recently, the secrets regarding God's kingdoms were shrouded in mystery, ambiguity, half truths due to misinformation, absence of true knowledge or involved persecution. Recently, however, since 1967, major transformations have occurred. More and more of His kingdoms are revealed (1, 2). In addition, new information presented is in a clearer, more easily understood language than before, therefore, one does not have to second guess the intent of the authors of this material.

In life, or in nature, if one scrutinizes only a few observations of any phenomenon (called data points), it would be difficult to draw any conclusions regarding these observations. However, this readily changes as more and more observations are made, as more data are gathered. Definitive conclusions regarding these data can now be made. A similar type of assessment can be made regarding pathways to God based on recently available information.

Nineteen sixty seven was a pivotal year for God awareness because of two reasons. First, as mentioned before, awareness of a third major pathway to God surfaced that existed from time immemorial but which remained largely hidden. This is Advanced religion, Eckankar, or Spirituality (3) that now supplemented two

5

already fairly known existing ones, namely, intellectualism, and the psychic pathway (Old-age and modern religions, yoga, mysticism, and others).

However, the model that prepares one for the Intellectual and Psychic pathways is far different than the one that prepares one for the Spiritual pathway.

Second, information mentioned above that was presented in 1967 suggested the need for an urgent reevaluation of some commonly accepted notions regarding God and His kingdoms.

Now, it has become abundantly clear that life does not begin in the cradle nor end at the grave: after death, one does not resurrect from the grave at the second coming of Christ (4); resurrection is not of the physical body but involves the spiritual body (4); Jehovah is not God but an assistant to God (3), and one does not possess a Soul but is Soul (5).

The latter is the divine part of each of us that is obtained from God. However, many individuals do not know this. Therefore, one must strive to find this part of one's self and recognize it.

Some traditions and recent information by Paul Twitchell (3) and Harold Klemp (6) state that we are Soul, albeit immature, created by God and sent to the earth (eventually encased in a body), and elsewhere-our temporary homes-in order to seek and obtain an education and spiritual maturity. The purpose of this training is to become Co-workers with God (6).

It may be a surprise to learn that each of us has three educational paths to pursue, if not already pursued. As said earlier, these are the Intellectual, or objective, that can take one one-sixth of the way into God's kingdoms: the Psychic, or subjective, that prepares one for almost half of this journey; and the Spiritual, also subjective, that has the potential to reach all the way into God's kingdoms.

These three pathways provide information and experiences for Co-workership internships with God. However, the degree and extent of one's Co-workership training will depend on the number of pathways one has pursued over time. If only one pathway were pursued, then the experiences received will not be as extensive as if two or even three pathways were studied in a serious manner. Therefore, for a large majority of individuals, their education may be incomplete.

Intellectual training, pursued at our own pace, allows us to obtain the requisite training and experience, secure employment, raise a family if desired, and seek appropriate rest and relaxation.

On the other hand, psychic training, to a certain extent, and spiritual training (Advanced religion) allow us to return to God's kingdoms, our true home, also at our own pace. However, many persons do not realize that old-age and modern religions, and other studies, components of the psychic since they are largely subjective, are not the only pathway in returning home to God, neither are they the fastest.

Today, these training systems are used in gathering and processing information. Furthermore, these systems, to varying degrees, employ the intellect, that is, thinking which is facilitated through use of the brain, the mind, the physical senses (seeing, hearing, feeling, smelling, and tasting), as well as the bodily systems. These are the circulatory, digestive, excretory, genetic, immune, integumentary, lymphatic, muscular, nervous, reproductive, respiratory, skeletal, and urinary systems (7, 8)

The nervous and muscular systems, for example, allow not only reception of a stimulus (such as a sound to the ear), but, also, possible movement as a reaction to this stimulus in an attempt to localize this sound. Of course, the circulatory and digestive systems, respectively, convey to and supply the appropriate muscles with energy in the blood in order to facilitate this movement.

The human body which integrates all bodily systems is literally the house, or apartment, in which Soul resides while one is alive on earth, and from which Soul leaves temporarily and returns during sleep, or vacates permanently at death of the body. Soul is immortal (2). A large majority of humanity uses the Intellectual system that is one major pathway to God.

The Psychic and Spiritual systems, on the other hand, have additional features at their disposal that can augment the data that are obtained by the Intellectual pathway. Although these systems in total feature at least eight major options for getting into God's kingdoms, the differences among these pathways relate to one's level of awareness (consciousness).

Although one can rank order these pathways from the lowest to the highest, based on the level of awareness attained, the recognition that each individual has the right to choose his/her own pathway is paramount.

Furthermore, an individual's interpretation of information relating to a particular pathway will be always correct, based on this person's level of awareness. For example, an individual who claims that two plus two equal five is correct based on this person's level of consciousness (awareness). It is quite possible, however, that such a person may have found a unique method of mathematical addition.

It appears that pathways to God's kingdoms probably developed as various options over time as mankind evolved from ancient times to modern times, from limited intellectual thinking to more advanced thinking, from lesser awareness of God's works to greater awareness and understanding. The Intellectual, Psychic, and Spiritual systems will be discussed in Chapters 5-8.

Many persons readily accept information on the arts, science, or technology obtained by the Intellectual system, but baulk, even hem and haw, when data gathered from psychic and spiritual investigations are presented. The former individuals claim that this psychic or spiritual information is contrary to what their parents and grandparents taught them and is thus contrary to God's word. Further, they claim that if this information is not found in the Christian bible, then it is not the truth, as if the Christian bible were the sole dispenser of spiritual wisdom.

Others feel that if new information on God does not fit into their belief system, then such information is not worthy of their consideration. It appears that a study of history shows that new information is always forthcoming.

Therefore, the individuals mentioned immediately above should ask the question, "Is there information on God that exists of which I am unaware?" Ironically, it is the right of each individual to select the type of information that he/she wishes to examine.

Some individuals, especially scientists, feel that if data on God cannot be tested in a scientific laboratory, then they are unreliable or do not exist. Data regarding the origin of life on earth will be discussed in Chapter 5.

If you feel quite fervently that Jehovah, Buddha, or Jesus is God, then this book may not be for you. Similarly, if your interpretation of the Trinity (the Father, Son, Holy Ghost concept) makes Jesus (the Son) equal in stature to God (the Father), then there is a strong possibility that this interpretation of the Trinity is not the correct one (9).

Do you believe that the devil is a teacher selected by God? No? Then maybe there is a need to read on to discover whether he is, or is not (10). If indeed he is an educator, do you have the muster to pass his classes regarding the five passions of the mind depicted by the acronym, vagal (vanity, anger, greed, attachment to material possessions, and lust)?-(11).

What of the concept of Spiritual Masters?, one may ask (12). Or, a Living Teacher or Living ECK Master?-(12). "Did you say correctly a Living Teacher?" Whoever heard of him? is often heard when this name is mentioned. Have you heard of chakras (13, 14), or Soul Travel?-(15).

Finally, is it possible that while living in the human body one can cross the border of death in full consciousness and return to tell the tale (at least privately, not publicly)?

The Intellectual pathway, the first of those leading back into God's kingdoms introduces the inner operation of His kingdoms by means of the laws of Physics, Chemistry, Biology, Mathematics, interactions among social beings including man, economic forces that interplay with our lives, energy, matter, space, time, and so on.

The Intellectual pathway allows one to trace one's ancestry back in time. However, it has limitations regarding one's life in previous incarnations. Advanced elements of the Psychic pathway, in a limited way, and the Spiritual pathway, in a complete manner, can provide this information from previous incarnations.

If interested in other pathways back to God and some of the topics mentioned above, an examination of the transition from intellectual, to psychic, and spiritual thinking and practice may be informative. The intellectual, psychic, then spiritual training should allow one to find one's way back into God's kingdoms on one's own after initial assistance. That is a very tall order. The term, Spiritual pathway, mentioned here refers to an Advanced religion called Eckankar (see Chapter 8).

3

God's Kingdoms, Karma and Reincarnation

Harold Klemp (16) commented recently that Saint Paul knew of someone who was lifted up into the third heaven. This presupposed a first and second heaven. By extension, one can ask the question, "How many heavens actually exist?"

Paul Twitchell (11) answered this question by stating that God's kingdoms currently consist of numerous heavens or planes of existence beyond twelve, but lists only twelve. Furthermore, God's universes are still expanding. See the following references for presentation of these planes of existence (11, 36).

The planes of God are subdivided into two major divisions, namely, the psychic division (planes 1-4) and the spiritual component (planes 5-12, and above). Each plane in each division is run by an administrative hierarchy, the chief of which is a sub-God (a Governor or Ruler) - (11, 36).

The sub-Gods of planes 1-4 are Elam, Jot Niranjan or Jehovah, Ramkar, and Omkar, in that order (36). Planes 5-12 also have sub-Gods. Plane 12 is God's residence. Some persons feel that God is neither masculine nor feminine (11), therefore, the appellation It is used (11).

Access to the planes of God is not as one would expect. Most persons look outwardly in an effort to find God, believing that lavish churches, temples, and synagogues will entice him here to earth. These individuals do not fully realize that access to the kingdoms of God is in the opposite direction, namely, inwardly.

Of note is that each plane can be entered in contemplation by means of a password (11, 36). Furthermore, each plane features elements that must be mastered before one can proceed to the plane above. For plane 1, the earth and the rest of the physical universe, one must master the five passions of the mind depicted by the acronym, vagal-vanity, anger, greed, attachment to material possessions, and lust (11, 36).

Trying to abolish these passions outright may be a difficult task. The Living Master recommends that one substitute each passion with its opposite. Fear, also, can hinder progress into the planes. Planes 2, and 3, in that order, are those of emotions, and former lives. While God communicates with us by means of the Light and Sound, the Living Master in each age is the only one who can provide us with this linkup.

Twitchell (11) comments that planes 1-4, run by the devil, are the negative pole of God's worlds, while plane 5 is the positive pole. Planes 1-4 contain matter in density in an inverse relationship. The matter on earth (plane 1) is denser than that on plane 4 (the Mental world) – see also reference 36.

Two other points should be made about the planes. First, planes 1-4 are ones of duality. Here, there is light and its counterpart, darkness. Where there is love, the opposite, hate, exists. There may be a reason for the planes of duality. Planes 1-4 exhibit time and space. Therefore, planes 1-4 must be mastered and duality experienced in order to understand those planes where duality, as well as time and space, do not exist, as seen on plane 5, and above (11, 36).

Second, the planes are also associated with Light and Sound, the voice of God (11, 36). The sound of thunder heard in contemplation indicates plane 1; while the sound of a flute originates from plane 5 (11, 36). Also, blue is the color of the Mental plane (plane 4); whereas pink indicates the Astral plane (plane 2)-(11).

There are many techniques that are observed in various schools for getting into the planes. Some schools can only take one to plane 4 believing that this is the highest plane attainable. In addition, use of the mechanism of the mind alone can only take one to plane 4. To go any further, the Soul mechanism must be employed.

Furthermore, the time that it takes to get into the planes varies with each school. The fastest method known today is observed in Advanced religion (Eckankar), or Spirituality-see Chapter 8. Training to get into God's kingdoms is more rigorous than intellectual training.

Teacher types in God's kingdoms vary with the type of pathway that is being pursued. In the Intellectual pathway, instructors, teachers, assistant-, associate-, and full professors as well as research professors are encountered. For the Psychic pathway, one observes masters of different grades. On the other hand, Spiritual masters and a Living Master (Living ECK Master) are unique to the Spiritual pathway and can lead one to the plane where God resides.

After God created Soul, and after intense observation of its actions, the Creator realized that Soul needed training in order to become a Co-worker. Hence, segments of the upper worlds (planes 5-11) and the lower worlds (planes 1-4) were created for Soul's training. Soul was then temporarily banished to the earth in order that It receive training in God's works so that It could find its way back home (plane 12).

Homing beacons for Soul were established. These are the Sound, the Light, and the Wayshower, the guide who is the Living Master-(10, 11). To qualify as a Living Master, one must be able to operate on earth as well as in God's other kingdoms.

As said earlier, the sound heard in contemplation tells Soul how far it is from home base (plane 12). For example, the sound of thunder tells Soul that it is still on plane 1; whereas, a sound of a flute indicates quite a way to go for one is on plane 5 (11, 36), close, but not close enough. In a similar fashion, the light seen represents progress towards plane 12. Pink indicates plane 2 (the Astral world), blue, plane 4 (the Mental world), and orange, plane 3 (the Causal world)-(11).

The curriculum for a segment of Soul's training in the lower worlds is provided by the devil, appointed by God for teaching purposes. In order to begin its experiences, Soul was given a start-up karma, termed Adi Karma by the Lords of Karma (17). Soul had to choose from the five passions of the mind (vanity, anger, greed, attachment to material possessions, and lust-(11), short straws, or the five opposites (humility, gentleness, satisfaction, non-attachment, and desirelessness)-long straws.

Apparently the system worked this way. If Soul drew a short straw and selected anger, sometime during its life, more likely in adolescence, a serious altercation picked by this individual could result in serious injury to itself. The result can be a quick attitudinal shift to peacefulness. Not only did this Soul pick up some karma, but also, some experience as well. Its anger can now be tamed.

On the other hand, another Soul might choose a long straw, and select non-attachment to material possesions. Although the renter of a beautiful home with a magnificent garden, this individual did not see the benefit of purchasing a garden hose. Unfortunately, when a fire accidentally broke out in the house, it could not be saved due to the absence of a garden hose. This Soul also picked up some experience because of the event above, but probably realized that essential material goods are of some benefit.

Sooner or later, Soul begins to realize that karma is not punitive and laced with hate, but corrective and administered with love. Karma is a universal law that binds all life (human, animal, plant, mineral)-(17).

Karma results from violation of spiritual law by either thought, word, or deed. Four types of karma exist, namely, Adi Karma, or primal karma, that aids in securing initial experience. Second is Fate karma, earned in a previous life that serves as a foundation for the present life. Third is Reserve Karma, while Daily Karma is fourth (17).

In life, one should constantly maintain and monitor one's balance sheet. Substitute a bad deed with a good one. If a recipient of some benefit, be a donor.

Karma was discussed above. But what has karma to do with reincarnation? As a result of karma, three things can follow: present or future benefits (good karma), present or future liabilities (bad karma), or no karma due to karmaless action that was taken (18).

Reincarnation is repeated rebirths over time. Some call it a birth, death, birth, death cycle. However, since Soul is immortal, the better expression can be birth, translation, birth, translation, using a term used in Advanced Religion (Eckankar) when Soul leaves the body permanently (19).

Reincarnation appears to be needed for two reasons. First, it serves to eliminate good or bad karma. Second, with all there is to know in order to be a Co-worker with God, multiple lifetimes are needed in an effort to master this material. However, during this process of learning, more and more karma can accumulate through violation of spiritual law.

This cycle of repeated birth, translation, birth, translation, is termed The Wheel of the Eighty Four (17). For Soul, this involves passing seven times through the Zodiacal circle, spending one hundred thousand years (one lac) in each Zodiacal sign (17). Eighty four lacs amount to eight million, four hundred thousand years (17). If Soul's karma calls for it, It has to make this tiresome journey. On the other hand, escape from this wheel involves meeting the Living Master and accepting him (17)-see Chapter 8.

Finally, karmaless action can result from doing everything in the name of God, or Its representative here on earth, the Living Master (17, 18)-Chapter 8. This ensures escape from karma and its rounds of rebirths (17). The quest for karmaless action is especially applicable to health care professionals who can easily pick up a patient's karma. Illness results from violation of spiritual law, knowingly, or unknowingly.

4

Pathways into God's Kingdoms

Many persons view old-age and modern religions as the only pathway into God's kingdoms. Little do they realize that other pathways exist; furthermore, some are more advanced than old-age and modern religions based on how far into God's kingdoms one can reach.

Table 1 presents eight options than can be condensed into three major categories, namely, the Intellectual, the Psychic, and the Spiritual. As said earlier, each of these groups has three subgroups, namely, the elementary, the intermediate, and the advanced.

The psychic sub-groups include the elementary (old-age and modern religions), the intermediate (elementary yoga as well as others), and the advanced (mysticism and advanced yoga).

An attempt is made to rank-order these pathways based on how close to God one can get. What is presented is a best guesstimate for some pathways.

Intellectual pathways are intellectualism itself as seen in scientific and other thinking methods, and atheism.

The psychic pathway features the black arts, old-age and modern religions, agnosticism, independent workers as well as mysticism. Spirituality (Advanced religion) is featured as a new-age religion, Eckankar. A brief description of each of these categories follows.

God-Related Activity	Maximum Possible Plane Reached	Frequency of Activity	Pathway type	Mechanism of Action
8. Advanced Religion#	12 plus	Daily	Spiritual	Advanced subjective experimentation, Soul Travel
7. Mysticism and yoga+	2-4	Daily	Advanced Psychic	Subjective experimentation, Astral Travel
6. Independent Worker	Unknown	Unknown	Psychic	Unknown
5. Agnosticism	2-4	Unknown	Psychic	Unknown
4. Old-Age and Modern Religion	2-4*	Weekly	Elem. psychic	Prayer, singing, chanting, dancing and feasting
3. The black arts	Unknown	Unknown	Psychic	Unknown
2. Atheism	2	Unknown	Intellectual	Unknown
1. Intellectualism	2	Daily to weekly	Intellectual	Objective experimentation

Table 1 – Pathways into God's kingdoms.
*Plane 2 for the congegration; #Eckankar or Spirituality; +Intermediate and advanced psychic.

Intellectualism supports the view that mankind can solve problems using scientific approaches, but not necessarily by science alone. Here, God plays a minor role in one's evolution.

An atheist does not believe that God exists. However, some war veterans will state quite emphatically that there are no atheists in a foxhole. It is quite possible that an atheist was once a member of old-age and modern religions and was turned off by its teachings. Members of all two groups named above probably cannot reach higher than plane 2, the Astral plane.

Individuals in the intellectual category generally use the objective senses, in contrast with the subjective senses. Use of the objective senses involves employment of the mind, the brain, and the five external senses of sight, hearing, touch, feeling, and smell. On the other hand, use of the subjective senses, as seen in the psychic and spiritual pathways, involves the brain, the five inner senses of sight, hearing, touch, feeling, and smell as well as the mind. In addition, the Spiritual pathway also uses the Soul mechanism. In an effort to turn on the inner senses, the eyes generally are closed. Chapter 5 discusses aspects of the intellectual pathway.

In the psychic group will be found the black arts, old-age and modern religions, agnosticism, independent workers, yoga and mysticism.

The black arts, called "high science" by some, feature black magic, some witchcraft, voodoo, obeah, Satanism, and others, and is directed by the devil, one of God's directors. As a teacher, terrible consequences can result for those who fail the devil's exams.

According to Twitchell (11), twelve major religions to God exist, all originating from the Holy Spirit. These are Animism, Buddhism, Christianity, Hinduism, Islamism, Jainism, Mystery Cults, Shintoism, Sufism, Taoism, and Zoroastrianism (11). From this list, it is preferable to designate Mystery Cults under Mysticism, a segment of the psychic pathway (see Chapters 6 and 7).

Additional discussions on old-age and modern religions will be found in Chapter 6. In addition, numerous offshoots of old-age and modern religions for the congregation will be discussed in Chapter 6.

The agnostic believes in God but does not feel that God can really be known. Truths regarding God may have eluded this individual. A pathway change may be needed in this instance.

The independent worker, for want of a better term, is a unique individual. This person believes in God and thinks that he/she already possesses the knowledge that is needed to find God. The feeling here is that no outside assistance is necessary. This person certainly has not heard of the Living Master.

The path called Mysticism features numerous groups such as Yoga (13, 14), Theosophy (20), Rosicrucianism (21-24), and the Society of the Golden Dawn, to name a few. Some aspects of Yoga and Rosicrucianism will be discussed in Chapter 7.

The spiritual pathway is one of Advanced religion, such as Eckankar. Among other factors, Advanced religion differs from old-age and modern religions due to the location of the seat of power for each type, as well as the presence of a Living Master in Advanced religion but not in old-age and modern religions (see Chapter 8).

Among the aspirants to God's kingdoms pursuing the three major pathways, namely, the Intellectual, the Psychic, or the Spiritual, one can find two types of individuals. These are the stationary type and the mobile type (Figure 1). The stationary type of individual is convinced that a particular pathway is the correct one and, therefore, literally plants both feet firmly on that pathway-see A, C, and E in Figure 1.

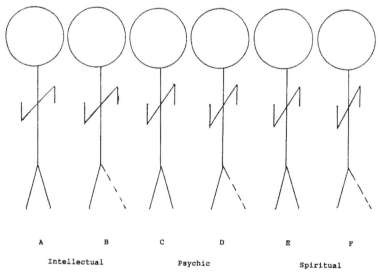

A	B	C	D	E	F
Intellectual		Psychic		Spiritual	

Figure 1 – Action Steps to be Taken in the Pursuit of God.

On the other hand, mobile individuals B, D, and F are constantly looking for better ways to reach God. Individual B, or D, respectively, may keep both feet on the Intellectual, and Psychic pathways, in that order, for a time unsure of where to go, eventually staying put or moving on to the Psychic, or Spiritual pathway, in that order.

Some individuals who pursue a pathway change do not make a clean break from their previous pathway. Instead, they may delay this effort unsure of whether to go forward, stay put, or go backward. Thus, their spiritual energies are diluted through focus on the previous as well as the present pathway.

It is interesting to note that some persons in the Spiritual, and most advanced pathway (Eckankar)-based on how far into God's kingdoms one can reach-do not recognize this for what it is worth and either revert back to the Psychic pathway, or to the Intellectual pathway. Unfortunately, such individuals may eventually continue where they left off, but in another lifetime. This can be termed an unrecognized missed opportunity.

The Intellectual, Psychic, and Spiritual pathways, in that order, will be discussed in greater detail in Chapters 5, 6-7 (for the psychic pathways), and 8 (for the Spiritual pathway). No further discussion will be made of the black arts, atheism, agnosticism, and the independent worker. The discussion on mysticism will examine elementary and intermediate yoga and some aspects of Rosicrucianism.

Which pathway is best for an individual? This question can be directed to the writer or to the reader. If the reader, then it is that individual's call.

Finally, as one proceeds from the Intellectual, to the Psychic, and then to the Spiritual pathway, less pomp and ceremony are observed.

5

The Intellectual Pathway

Any activity that employs the mind is intellectual. However, in this chapter, the statement above will be used when the mind and the five physical senses are used exclusively in evaluating information (objective techniques) at the expense of other enhancing methods that are available (subjective techniques).

The Intellectual pathway as seen today did not exist in this form in the past. It was elementary and gradually evolved with time to its present form.

Early mankind developed the ability to use fire for warmth and food preparation: fashioned tools for hunting and protection; and promoted communication and trading through use of an alphabet and numerical system.

Much later, other intellectual pursuits included classifying plants and animals: the discovery of steam; and assembling the elements into a periodic table.

Still later, unleashing forces from the atom, as well as examination of social, economic, health, and political forces that impacted on our well being followed. These resulted in improved living standards.

Humans, as well as other living things are Soul, a particle of God (3, 5, 6). The Soul of an individual must have self-recognition features in order to distinguish itself from other Souls.

The human body is literally the temple, house, or apartment in which Soul resides while on earth; therefore, every effort should be made to ensure that this structure is well maintained and functioning maximally. The intellect is a product of human thinking; therefore, equal effort should be made to provide the body with adequate nutrition, rest, relaxation, and exercise. Mitochondria in the cell contribute to the body's energy bank.

Furthermore, regular exercise increases the number of mitochondria. This translates to increased energy reserves that can be tapped in an emergency when increased energy is needed.

Also, exercise serves another purpose. One has a reference point regarding how the body should feel and react when well. This information should be useful when ill in an effort to restore health. Toxic or harmful materials should be avoided, especially recreational drugs, tobacco, and alcohol.

Harmonious interrelationships among the bodily systems favor greater efficiency of this machine. These systems were mentioned earlier.

In addition, proper functioning of the five physical senses, as well as the brain, mind, and spinal cord promote high-quality experiences. Disease states can reduce meaningful experiences considerably.

Furthermore, as Soul, one should endeavor to respect all spiritual laws since accidental, or deliberate violation of these by thought, word, or deed, can ultimately produce disease.

Soul was sent to earth to receive training and experiences in order to be an efficient Co-worker with God (6). Soul's quest here is to seek near-total awareness (consciousness).

Intellectual training exists at three levels (the elementary, intermediate, and advanced) and begins in kindergarden, and proceeds, sequentially to primary, middle (secondary), then high school, if one is so inclined. Additional steps in this training include college or university, technical school, professional school, or graduate school.

The training begins by learning to read, write, reason, and communicate, and ends with specialization in a particular discipline, if desired. This training provides increasing levels of experiences and awareness and can be both varied and extensive with choices from among multiple disciplines. These include art to engineering, medicine to technology, as well as aviation to environmental sciences. These experiences can be hands-on and quite meaningful in the quest for near-total awareness, as steps are made from the intellectual, to the psychic, and then to the spiritual. See reference 25 for intellectual preparation for the sciences.

One should realize that short-circuiting intellectual training by dropping out of some of these sequential steps, for example, high school, can reduce one's level of awareness and experiences. At the intellectual level, some training in God awareness is also provided but is limited in scope when compared with what can be achieved (see Chapters 6-8).

As said earlier, the Intellectual pathway introduces the inner workings of God's kingdoms by means of physical, biological, environmental and other disciplines through an examination of matter, energy, time, space, and other relevant laws.

Since the range of intellectual experiences is so extensive involving multiple disciplines that must be mastered, the need for multiple lifetimes (reincarnation) in order to achieve even a modicum of success suggests itself.

Various methods and techniques are used in order to stimulate intellectual thinking. Of these, the scientific method is most prominently used today. This is an objective method, not a subjective one. The five physical senses are employed at the expense of the five spiritual senses.

The scientific method consists of five major steps, namely, an observation, a question, a hypothesis, experimentation in order to test the hypothesis and attempt to answer the question, and a theory or law. The observation is the phenomenon under scrutiny; while the question is asked next and can be a who?, why?, what?, when?, where?, or how? variety.

Furthermore, the question asked must be relevant and testable. The hypothesis is an educated guess regarding a possible answer to the question asked. An experiment is designed in an effort to answer the question under consideration; while analysis of data obtained from the experiment allows formulation of a theory, or law.

The scientific method employs the mind and the five physical senses. Its use should be independent of the experimenter's opinions (thus objective in nature). However, a German scientist, Kekule (26) experimenting with a substance in Organic Chemistry, had conflicting data from two sources. One set of data suggested that the substance under study was linked as a chain, while other data suggested otherwise.

Thereupon, this scientist sat before his fireplace in an armchair and dozed off, thus turning off the objective consciousness and turning on the subjective. Then he dreamt of a snake biting its own tail. Upon awakening, he realized that the substance under study was ring-shaped. This structure, Benzene, turned out to be the parent compound of many ring-shaped structures of tremendous biological importance.

In this instance, the scientific community tacitly accepted information that was obtained by the subjective method. Unfortunately, they did not explore further the ability of the latter method in gathering information largely because of the absence of the techniques that are involved.

The scientific method allows the systematic gathering and analysis of data better than any other method of inquiry known today. Although an objective method, it easily lends itself, with modification, to analysis of subjective data as seen in psychic, and spiritual inquiries (see Chapters 7-8).

The scientific method can also be used to trace the evolution or progression of life on earth, and can be useful in supporting the theory of reincarnation. Many believe that early life evolved as a single cell, then multiple cells, tissues, organs, and organ systems, as seen in humans. During this process, invertebrates (organisms without a vertebral column) were seen, then vertebrates (organisms with a vertebral column), as observed in fishes, amphibians, reptiles, birds, and mammals (as humans).

It is a daunting task to trace the evolution of invertebrates from a single cell. However, for the vertebrates, evidence is mounting that mankind evolved from fishes way back in time. For example, a study of Comparative Anatomy and Embryology reveals that during the early embryonic development of fishes, amphibians, reptiles, birds, and mammals (includes humans), structures from fishes (such as gill arches) often persist in humans as fistulas, or are incorporated into jaw structures (27, 28).

The human kidney also demonstrates such evolutionary trends, proceeding from a primitive form in fishes (the pronephros) to the advanced human pattern (the metanephros)-(27, 28).

The intellectual type of individual often rejects information on psychic or spiritual matters because upon examining his/her computer (the brain) for such data, a blank is drawn. Then panic results. Thus rejection of these types of data appears to be a safety device. Use of the mechanisms of the mind solely in thinking presents limitations.

Furthermore, this type of individual has not heard of, or may be fearful of using such techniques as concentration, meditation, or contemplation, to name a few.

In addition, the use of such techniques do not readily yield instant results. Intelligence, then, might not be the best measure of ranking one's knowledge, but awareness.

The Intellectual pathway allows a study of matter, energy, time, space, and relevant laws in areas where these exist (planes 1-4, Chapter 2), and thus provide a background for later study where such phenomena are not observed (planes 5, and above, Chapter 2).

Furthermore, dualities studied, for example, light contrasted with darkness, or pain with absence of pain, advance an understanding of these qualities better than if only one quality of any substance existed, where there is absence of duality.

God's kingdoms were presented in Chapter 2. How far into His kingdoms can the Intellectual pathway take an individual? Most likely, to the Astral Plane as home base unless this person meets with a Spiritual Master, the Living Master, or has latent previous psychic, or spiritual experiences, or current ones. However, temporary visits to the Mental Plane can be made at the discretion of the masters mentioned above.

Finally, at the risk of sounding redundant, the Nobel laureate of the Intellectual pathway is the Nobel laureate. On the other hand, the "Nobel laureate" of the spiritual pathway is the Living Master.

6

The Psychic Pathway-Old-Age and Modern Religions

The path to God called religion, a largely subjective route, consists of three components, namely, Old-age, Modern, and an advanced component called Spirituality (Eckankar)-(Chapter 8). The difference between the three lies in their headquarters in the spiritual kingdom. The seat of Old-age and Modern religions is on the Mental Plane (the fourth plane) under the jurisdiction of the devil; whereas the Soul Plane (the fifth plane) houses Advanced religion (Spirituality)-see Chapter 2.

Like the Intellectual pathway, the Psychic pathway also has undergone evolutionary changes as mankind sought to understand his God, as well as control the forces of nature. Here, the priesthood played a prominent role. Yet, many individuals did not, and still do not, recognize that elementary, intermediate and advanced psychic paths such as Yoga and Mysticism, (e.g., Rosicrucianism), respectively, exist.

Old-age and modern religions are psychic since subjective techniques are used. However, since they are elementary psychic, this pathway to God is on the fringe of the margins of possible psychic experiences so that when some, if not all members of the congregation, close their eyes, experiences are not forthcoming since they do not know what to do next. Some even use this time to take a nap.

Lack of results occurs when faith substitutes for experiences that can be obtained from experimentation. Some members of the congregation in old-age and modern religions do have subjective experiences when in a trance. However, such individuals cannot consciously recall such events.

Each type of religion, Old-age, Modern, and Advanced consists of an outer (exoteric) and an inner (esoteric) segment. The exoteric segment is generally for the congregation, or beginning students (a group activity), while the esoteric is for the priesthood, or advanced students (a largely individual activity). Spirituality (Advanced religion or Eckankar) will be discussed in Chapter 8.

The discussion on religions will focus on techniques that are used by the congregation rather than the priesthood. Religions are largely subjective, as stated before; however, Old-age and Modern religions use the subjective senses in an elementary manner and not in the way that these are used in Mysticism (Chapter 7), or Spirituality (Chapter 8). Religions are thus psychic in nature, although not very high on the psychic scale for members of the congregation, when compared with other psychic pathways such as Mysticism (Chapter 8).

In Old-age and Modern religions for the congregation, there is little, if any, experimentation seen in an effort to seek God and Its kingdoms beyond singing, dancing, prayer, chanting, and feasting, and even these are not structured for the collection and analysis of data. As mentioned earlier, the only quasi-experiments that are observed here involve trance-like experiences in which the participant is not conscious of events that occur.

If one has an unknown seed and wishes to find out its identity, what should be done? Can one rely on faith to find the answer? No. One has to experiment by planting the seed in fertile soil and observe the kind of plant or tree that emerges.

This same principle applies to Old-Age and Modern religions. It will be seen later in this book that intermediate and advanced psychic studies as well as Spirituality feature many experiments in an effort to convert belief to knowledge. The writer does not want to convey the impression that faith is not important. It is quite important but should be considered a first step. Experimentation should follow (see Chapter 8 also).

Twitchell (11) presented eleven major religions as well as mystery cults, all originating from the Holy Spirit. These religions and mystery cults are developed by God to fit the needs of all individuals, at all different levels of awareness (consciousness). They also provide viable options for Soul to eventually find its way back into God's kingdoms. Religions have many subgroups (see below).

Barrett et al. (29) reported that there are 10,000 distinct religions worldwide. Adherents.com (30) believes that religions can be categorized as classical (12 groups), based on size (9 groups), or functionally oriented, but still classical (11 groups).

Based on size, Adherents.com (30) presented 22 major religions listed in an inverse relationship. Christianity, by approximate estimates, has the largest number of adherents (2.1 billion), while Scientology has the least (500,000).

Adherents.com (30) feels that the religions listed in Table 2 represent over 98% of the world's population. Not listed in Table 2 are religions such as Mandeans, PL Kyodan, Ch'ondogyo, Vodoun (or Voodoo), New Age, Seicho-No-le, Falun Dafa/Falun Gong, Taoism, and Roma (30).

Christianity consists of over 40 sub-groups that include Catholics, Anglicans, Seventh-Day Adventists, Baptists, Lutherans, and Methodists (30). In addition, sub-groups in Islam feature Sunni, Shi'ite, and Sufis (30). Furthermore, Santeria, Candomble, Vodoun, and Shango are part of African Diasporic religions (30).

Over the years, many, if not all, religions have lost the essential flavor of God's message-that its communication with all members involves varying aspects of Light and Sound, depending on how far one has reached into His kingdoms while still living (11).

Because of absence of awareness (consciousness), many religions, or their sub-groups, view Jehovah, Krisna, Buddha, and Jesus as God. Some religions do recognize Jesus and Mohammed as messengers of God. Furthermore, Jesus is given the same status as God when the Trinity (the Father, Son, Holy Ghost concept) is interpreted by some. This is not correct.

1. Christianity.	12. Judaism.
2. Islam.	13. Baha'i.
3. Secular/Nonreligious/Agnostic/Atheist.	14. Jainism.
4. Hinduism.	15. Shinto.
5. Chinese traditional.	16. Cao Dai.
6. Buddhism.	17. Zoroastrianism.
7. Primal indigenous.	18. Tenrikyo.
8. African traditional and diasporic.	19. Neopaganism.
9. Sikhism.	20. Unitarian-Universalism.
10. Juche.	21. Rastafarism.
11. Spiritism.	22. Scientology.

Table 2 – Major Religions of the World Ranked by Size. Abridged from Adherens.com (2005), and used with permission (30).

Moreover, the idea that a Saviour under all circumstances can relieve one of one's karmic responsibilities is promoted. Can a person who died and was buried really rise from the grave at Jesus' second coming? This does not appear to be a very elegant way to ensure continuity of life, disease free.

An increased awareness level regarding the event above would not only rule out the possibility of a second visit by Christ, but also, the possibility of a human body levitating from the grave at that time.

The reason is that we are Soul and the latter is immortal (9). The human body is a temporary mortal structure in which Soul resides when the body is alive and from which it vacates permanently at death (a translation)-see Chapter 8.

Furthermore, "resurrection is of the spiritual self, not the human body"-(4).

Most old-age and modern religions as part of their rituals offer prayers, vocalization (singing of hymns), repetition of mantras, the latter either as single words, or multiple words, fasting, feasting, and dancing.

Some prayers make demands of God as if He does not know the petitioner's needs. A prayer that closes with the words, "Thy will be done," should be a better way of petitioning God than one without these words (4). An even better prayer is to sing the word HU (4).

According to Harold Klemp (16), some hymns contain a holy name for God, HU-see Chapter 8. Hymns have the ability to change the congregations' mood from melancholic to euphoric, from hopelessness to hopefulness. The use of mantras (with or without prayer beads) in old-age and modern religions is less extensive here than in Mysticism, or Advanced Religion (Spirituality)- see Chapters 7-8.

Can the scientific method, with modification, be used to gather and analyze data in old-age and modern religions? Absolutely, even though one should expect greater variation in individuals when analyzing subjective data here when compared with objective data gathered by means of the intellectual method (Chapter 5).

In old-age and modern religions, prayer, singing, use of mantras, fasting, feasting, and dancing are not structured scientifically for data gathering and analysis. The efficacy of these techniques is not analyzed. Although miracles in healing do occur, they are random and unpredictable. Old-age and modern religions do not have as many experimental tools for gathering and evaluating elementary psychic data as does Mysticism, or Advanced religion (Spirituality)-see Chapters 7-8.

Missing, then from old-age and modern religions are experimental approaches to data collection and analysis (as seen in the Intellectual pathway) as well as an absence of a greater variety of questions that can be asked of God, or techniques mastered, but are not. This probably results from a decreased awareness level in old-age and modern religions when compared with that seen in Mysticism and Spirituality (Advanced religion).

Furthermore, old-age and modern religions do not ask the type of questions in depth and scope about God that Mysticism, or Spirituality does. Terms such as chakras, Soul Travel, or projections are unfamiliar ones (see Chapters 7-8).

Are old-age and modern religions needed today? Absolutely. Does everyone need these religions as a path to God? Maybe, maybe not; this is the individual's call.

Finally, since the headquarters of old-age and modern religions is on the Mental plane (11), it appears that it will be difficult for participants in these religions to go beyond this plane without the assistance of the Living Master or Spiritual Masters, who are cognizant of life beyond the fourth plane (see Chapters 7-8). Moreover, members of the congregation probably cannot go beyond the Astral (second) plane.

7

The Psychic Pathway-Mysticism

For those who do not wish to pursue the Intellectual pathway, old-age and modern religions, or intermediate psychic pathways for seeking God, Mysticism is a viable option. The latter allows the conversion of one's belief to knowledge by means of experimentation through application of the scientific method, with modification, that employs subjectivity instead of objectivity.

Like old-age and modern religions, and other psychic pathways, Mysticism is subjective, emphasizing greater use of the subjective senses (psychic vision, hearing, smelling, touching, and tasting) than do old-age and modern religions.

Mysticism uses the mind. However, the latter has limitations in reaching into God's kingdoms. The mind can only take one to the Mental (4th) plane. In order to go further, one needs to use the Soul mechanism. In endeavoring to reach the fourth floor (plane), one literally needs a four-stage booster rocket; whereas a five-stage booster stage is needed in order to get to floor (plane) five. The fuel for these rockets comes from doing the spiritual and other exercises (see Chapter 8). Additional boosts can come from the Living Master as well as Spiritual Masters.

The credo of most old-age and modern religions is very strong faith in a belief system. I believe in God the Father, I believe in this...I believe in that.

This is a necessary first step; however, the concept is not taken to the next logical step in order to find the truth about God, namely, experimentation, as said before.

The paradox here is that when God and Its agents are eventually found, one generally reverts to faith and trust, but in a master whom one may have met after initial experimentation. To repeat, experimentation allows the practitioner to separate knowledge from belief.

There is little, if any, experimentation involving the congregation that is observed in old-age and modern religions beyond prayer, singing, utilization of mantras, dancing, fasting, and feasting; and even these are not well designed nor show clear-cut definitive results in defining God and Its operations. As said earlier, in those instances in which a participant is in a trance-like state, loss of consciousness is observed.

On the other hand, profound experimentation is seen in Mysticism, and even more advanced experimentation is observed in Spirituality (Advanced religion)-see Chapter 8. Intermediate and advanced psychic experiments as well as experiments in Spirituality are no different than those seen in the Intellectual pathway. Examples of the latter include a housewife trying new ingredients when baking a cake, a gardener employing genetically-modified seeds in an effort to improve crop yield, or high school and college students experimenting in agriculture, biology, chemistry, mathematics, or physics. However, in the psychic and spiritual experiments, subjectivity substitutes for objectivity when experiments in the Intellectual pathway are compared.

Discussions on Mysticism follow, but first, some background information in order to understand the concepts of Mysticism.

Mysticism is a technique for reaching God that involves intuition, contemplation, and meditation (31). The ability to concentrate is indispensable for a mystical experience.

Training in Mysticism probably began in the mystery schools of all ages and in many countries. Pythagoras, the Greek mathematician, trained in Egyptian mystery schools and then took this knowledge to his home country where he operated a mystery school. Such schools also developed in countries such as Persia (modern-day Iran), India, and Tibet, to name a few. The Essenes were a mystical group in Jesus' day. In the period after Christ's death, the Gnostics taught God's mysteries but were persecuted.

Today, many groups teach about God and His kingdoms, and preliminary ways of getting there, based on their level of understanding. Such groups include the Rosicrucians, the Theosophical Society, the Society of the Golden Dawn, schools of yoga, and many others. The type and degree of instruction vary with each group.

In Mysticism, the goal is to exchange belief in a phenomenon with first-hand knowledge of the phenomenon studied. This is achieved by means of experimentation in a structured way.

Depending on the group, experiments on concentration, meditation, contemplation, chakra awakening, exteriorization of consciousness, elementary control of matter, analysis of auras, use of vowel sounds, development of intuition, and elementary dream analysis are pursued. Dreams can be good, bad, or ugly, but always informative.

Some groups use the yoga system exclusively, or some of its elements, in combination with their own system. Comments on a few of these topics mentioned immediately above follow.

Development of concentration can involve use of a candle flame safely, some bright object as a coin, or the tip of the nose. Meditation can be active, or passive. Contemplation can involve some prominent religious figure, or other figures as masters through use of visualization. Chakra awakening, under the guidance of a competent teacher, is vital for increasing one's awareness.

Chakras, more appropriately called psychic centers by the Rosicrucians, were mentioned in part around the second century according to the yoga practitioner and Shinto priest, Motoyama (14). The latter author traced the evolution of the early Indian literature on the chakras to the present.

Chakras are perceived clairvoyantly as discs of multicolored lights or as spokes of a wheel (13); and are reported to control energy channels termed nadis (of yoga) and meridians (of acupuncture)-(14). Motoyama (14) claims that in the physical body, the brain, nervous plexi, and acupuncture points represent the chakras; whereas the channels are depicted by the cardiovascular, lymphatic, and acupuncture meridian systems.

Chakras may be energy transfer and transformational centers involving the physical, astral, causal, and mental bodies as well. In all probability, each chakra receiving energy activates the underlying nervous plexus which in turn stimulates the appropriate endocrine gland to function.

Seven major chakras reportedly exist (13, 14) and, superiorly to inferiorly, are termed crown, brow, throat, heart, navel, spleen, and root by Leadbeater (13). Chakras are located over prominent nerve plexi. On the other hand, Twitchell (3) reported that six major chakras existed in the Physical, Astral, Causal, and Mental bodies, while only one existed in the Soul body.

Adept teachers strongly suggest that chakras be awakened in the proper sequence, and cautiously, otherwise harm can result.

Ozaniec (32) mentioned that a chakra spins due to the amount of energy in the system. Furthermore, by means of dowsing techniques, chakras on the left side of the body's center line produced clockwise energy patterns while those on the right side, counterclockwise motion. Disruption of this particular pattern indicated localized illness.

In the Eastern tradition, chakra awakening involves very rigid practices not suited to the undisciplined and weak at heart. In the Western world, however, less rigid practices are employed.

The awakening of chakras, though subjective, involves experimental procedures that should provide expected results, although not instantly initially. The time span in obtaining results here is much greater than that seen in the Intellectual pathway. Motoyama (14) presented experimental evidence in support of the existence of chakras, nadis, and meridians.

Mantras, or vowel sounds, as well as other exercises, as proper breathing, aid in chakra awakening.

In the Rosicrucian system, specific vowel sounds, uttered at specific frequencies, are used.

Psychic studies involving Mysticism deal with subtle energies called prana, or vital energy by the yogis, vital life force, and so on. These may very well be the Holy Spirit that is described in Spirituality (Advanced religion, or Eckankar)-see Chapter 8.

What abilities are developed by someone pursuing the mystical pathway? According to the literature, clairvoyance, clairaudience, psychic healing, levitation, to name a few. However, such an individual should endeavor to move on spiritually or risk being trapped in the worlds of matter (planes 1-4).

Furthermore, a psychic healer must take all necessary precautions in order not to take on a patient's karma; and must be cognizant of the fact that there is a spiritual reason for a patient's illness. Shortcircuiting a patient's karma without taking all necessary steps can transfer this karmic burden to the healer.

According to Motoyama (14), chakra awakening leads to enlightenment. Since life is continuous and involves evolutionary small steps, could chakra awakening and mastery of other mystical techniques be a final step in psychic development that can eventually lead, with adequate instruction, to a first step in Spirituality, the next pathway to God?

Twitchell (2) cautions that "The mystic is one who has never gone beyond the Mental worlds."

8

The Spiritual Pathway-Advanced Religion

The Spiritual pathway features Eckankar, a new-age religion that surfaced in 1965 under the direction of Paul Twitchell who was the Living Master (also called the Living ECK Master). Paul Twitchell was taught by Sirdar Singh, among others. Spirituality consists of an elementery, intermediate, and advanced component.

Eckankar (Advanced religion) is the highest spiritual organization known today, based on how far into God's kingdoms it can take an individual, because of the presence in this group of a Living Master. According to tradition, there can be only one Living Master in the world at any given period of history.

Eckankar is called an Advanced religion (Spirituality) since its headquarters is on the fifth (Soul) plane in contrast with that of old-age and modern religions whose headquarters is on the fourth plane under the guidance of the devil. Therefore, the teachings of Eckankar are undiluted.

Spirituality differs from old-age and modern religions also since the former conducts more structured experiments than the latter. In addition, since old-age and modern religions are psychic in nature, members of the congregation generally cannot go beyond the fourth plane when ready.

Furthermore, although Spirituality uses the mechanism of the mind initially (planes 1-4), it shifts to use of the Soul mechanism on plane 5 and above.

Many recognize the mind/physical body component of themselves but few the Soul/physical body part. Some do not even realize that the later exists. However, when they do, Self realization or one's recognition of one'self as Soul becomes prominent. This phenomenon occurs on Plane 5 (11).

Spirituality differs from Mysticism because of the psychic nature of the latter as well as restraints on its members, as seen in old-age and modern religions, for reaching beyond the fourth plane.

Spirituality uses the higher chakras exclusively when compared with Mysticism, and most important of all, Spirituality's guide, the Living Master, has tread the planes leading to God before and, therefore, is a competent guide for his students. He is a student's Personal Trainer, but in Soul Affairs. Although Spirituality initially takes its students through the psychic planes (1-4), its ultimate goal is the spiritual planes (5, and above).

It is unfortunate that from the cradle to the grave, many persons view old-age and modern religions as the only pathway to God, not being aware that Mysticism exists as well as Spirituality and a Living Master. Fortunate indeed, is one who has met the Living Master and recognizes him as the Master, Wayshower, or Godman. Who is this individual and what is his role in spiritual development?

As said earlier, in the beginning God sent immature Soul to the earth, and elsewhere, in order to secure an education, mature spiritually, and find its way back to His kingdoms in order to become a Co-worker (6). In its benevolence, God established three homing beacons to help Soul make the return journey safely. These are the Light, the Sound (together called the Holy Spirit), and the Living Master who can lead Soul back to God, whenever It is ready (10, 11).

The problem here is that some folks do not want to venture out temporarily just yet fearful that they may miss the backyard barbeques, sales at the shopping malls, yard sales, and the office parties. Others fear travelling to the other side believing that they might get lost and cannot return. "O ye of little faith?"-(33). The Living Master links one to the Light and Sound that emanate from God (4).

The Light varies in intensity as one ascends the planes; while the Sound is heard as variations, depending on the plane involved. For example, a single note of a flute heard in contemplation indicates that one has reached the fifth plane. God communicates with us by means of the Light and the Sound (4, 34).

Paul Twitchell died (translated) in 1971, and the mantle of the power of the Holy Spirit is currently in the hands of his successor, Sri Harold Klemp, the current Living Master. Sri is a title of respect, not worship (4).

The Living Master has assistance from many spiritual masters, many of whom served as living masters in their day. In the Trinity, the Living Master, the Son, acquires equality in consciousness with the Holy Spirit (the Holy Ghost), but not with God, the Father.

While Mysticism can take one to the fourth (Mental plane), and possibly to the fifth after numerous lifetimes, Spirituality, an advanced religion, can introduce a seeker to God (on Plane 12) by means of the Living Master in this lifetime. Spirituality is the shortest and fastest route to God's kingdoms (34). What does training in Spirituality involve?

The goal of the Living Master is to take his students through each plane, one by one, until God's residence is reached. According to Twitchell (1, 3), each plane is vibrant with many residents pursuing numerous activities. Passwords to each plane are learned. Eventually, each student can make these trips solo, although the watchful eye of the Living Master or other spiritual masters, is ever present.

The five passions of the mind (11) must be replaced with their opposites, humility instead of vanity, gentleness substituting for anger, satisfaction replacing greed, non-attachment to material things for attachment to material possessions, and desirelessness instead of lust, as stated earlier. Fear must be eliminated and substituted with trust in the Living Master. A student can seek assistance to see if a current problem has an anchor in the past.

Training in Spirituality for the congregation involves both exoteric and esoteric techniques. Featured are comprehensive dream analysis, concentration, contemplation, visualization, dream travel, Soul travel, as well as studies on karma and reincarnation.

In dream travel, a student can cross the barrier called death in full consciousness, visit the planes and return with recall of such events. In this way, not only can a student begin establishing himself/herself on these planes while living, but also, the fear of death can be eliminated now and when its time will be due. Soul travel involves expansion of awareness (consciousness)-(35).

In Spirituality, numerous daily exercises are performed in the conversion of belief to knowledge by means of experimentation. A modification of the scientific method in a subjective format is used.

The scientific method is useful for planes one to four, the worlds of matter, energy, time, and space. Here, however, Soul is restricted in its activities by the mind.

However, on planes five and above where time and space are nonexistent (2), where mind cannot operate since its activities are restricted beyond the Mental (fourth) plane, Soul's mechanism of action kicks in; the result is seeing, knowing, and being (34).

The holy book of Spirituality (Eckankar) is the *Shariyat-Ki-Sugmad (The Way of the Eternal)*. Two volumes of this book were transcribed recently by Paul Twitchell (2, 9, 11). About ten volumes await transcription (11). While there is an Old testament and a New testament in the Christian bible, the *Shariyat-Ki-Sugmad* can be considered a Newer testament, while the unpublished volumes can be named the Newest testament when they will be published.

The path called Spirituality (Eckankar) is not for the weak at heart, the fearful, the timid, or undisciplined. According to Harold Klemp (34), "the meek shall inherit the earth, but the strong shall inherit heaven," for here, one must be bold as an eagle, not timid as a dove (4). However, one quality of the meek, humility, as well as others such as divine love, are vital for entering the psychic or spiritual planes of God. Without love, no one "can enter into the heavenly kingdom (2)."

As said before, the Nobel laureate of the Intellectual pathway is the Nobel laureate. On the other hand, the "Nobel laureate" of the Spiritual pathway is the Living Master.

Spirituality presents one with the opportunity to acquire expanded awareness of God and His kingdoms far greater than one can imagine when the Intellectual, old-age and modern religious, and mystical pathways are compared. One can work for God either as a follower, or a leader. Spirituality presents one with the opportunity to acquire a leadership role through achievement of God Realization or awareness of God in this lifetime. If this is not achieved, one should at least try to achieve Self Realization, a specific awareness by aiming for and reaching the fifth plane.

In order to operate on earth, among other assets, one needs to develop the five physical senses. In a similar fashion, in order to function in the psychic and spiritual worlds, one needs to develop the spiritual senses. These assist in increasing awareness tremendously.

In an effort to nurture this awareness, a daily spiritual exercise is presented for opening the spiritual vision. This is as follows.

Sit comfortably in an armchair, back erect and palms down on each knee. With eyes closed, mentally focus on a spot between both eyebrows, about an inch below the skin. Take a deep breath for as long as is comfortable, hold it for a count of four, or less if necessary, then exhale while silently, or verbally, singing the word HU (pronounced hue) in a long drawn out fashion, also for as long as is comfortable.

While this is being done, visualize a spiritual person of your choice such as Jesus, Buddha, Mohammed, Paul Twitchell or Harold Klemp, the current Living Master. Repeat the instructions above for about two minutes, then wait for about five minutes passively for any result. If none, repeat the directions above. Stop this exercise after fifteen to twenty minutes unless some result is observed.

This experiment will allow one to test the hypothesis that access to God's kingdoms is from within, and not from without. In addition, if one can duplicate this experiment immediately, one month later, or even six months later, then this can convert an experience that some may consider my personal opinion into evidence of a phenomenon that can occur universally.

9

The Quest for Awareness

Recognition of the need during this lifetime for achieving total awareness (total consciousness), termed God realization (19), varies in a direct fashion as one progresses from the Intellectual, to the Psychic, then to the Spiritual pathway. Total awareness is associated with God-like qualities of omnipotence, omnipresence, and omniscience (19). Some persons have never heard of the concept of total awareness; while others may have but are unfamiliar with the steps that are needed in order to pursue it. Awareness results from activation of two mechanisms, that of the mind, and that of Soul (2).

Omnipotence, omnipresence, and omniscience are the goal of persons pursuing pathways to God; but are there preliminary, or intermediate, steps that are involved? Certainly.

The preliminary steps involve recognizing that there is awareness when awake and also awareness when asleep. How many persons know that they dream? Furthermore, what percentage of individuals recall their dreams? In addition, there is awareness when one pursues a single discipline, and even more awareness when one pursues multiple disciplines. The Intellectual pathway provides valuable information regarding God's kingdoms, such as analysis of matter, energy, physical and biological laws, as well as time and space. Other preliminary steps should alert one

Pathway to God	Possible Plane Reached	Type of consciousness Developed
3. Spiritual (Advanced religion, Eckankar)	12 plus	Ackshar
	12	God
	5	Self
2a. Advanced psychic, Mysticism, Advanced yoga	4	Cosmic
2b. Intermediate psychic, elementary yoga	2-4	Cosmic/Psychic
2c. Elementary psychic, Old-Age and Modern Religions	2*	Psychic
1. Intellectual	2	Human

Table 3 – Types of Awareness and God Planes Involved (11, 19).
*For the congregation only.

to the possibility that psychic and spiritual pathways also exist and can aid in the elevation of one's consciousness.

The intermediate or advanced Psychic pathway, through development of the chakras, concentration, meditation, and greater knowledge of God's kingdoms under the guidance of a competent teacher, could eventually lead to further development of awareness. Cosmic consciousness can be achieved (11, 36).

The Advanced religious pathway (Spirituality, or Eckankar), literally puts the icing on the cake when development of consciousness is concerned (Table 3 above). In this instance, one has the ability to achieve Eckshar (Cosmic) consciousness (11), Self consciousness (11, 19), God consciousness (19), as well as Ackshar consciousness (11, 19). Therefore, one should endeavor to spiritualize one's consciousness daily as one evolves through the following levels of awareness: human, non-intellectual, intellectual, Cosmic, Self, God, and Ackshar, in a direct manner, as one proceeds from the intellectual, to the psychic, then to the spiritual.

The recent rediscovery of a third major pathway to God that is more advanced than old-age and modern religions brings into the arena of awareness possible constitutional questions regarding separation of Church (meaning religion) and State. In light of the new information that was presented in this book, is reevaluation of this stricture in order?

The quest for God awareness must begin somewhere at the appropriate time, if not already pursued. The writer cannot prove to the reader the truths regarding the content of this book. Instead, one must toss the gauntlet to the reader with the expectation that the reader will accept the challenge to test the hypothesis presented earlier by means of experimentation.

As a start, the experiment presented before on the opening of the spiritual eye gives one the opportunity to test the hypothesis that God's kingdoms are within, not without.

In this book, an attempt is made to share recently discovered information regarding God and His kingdoms. It must be noted that information on God, and even on life itself, is not readily revealed. Huge time periods are involved as these data unfold. Seen is an evolution from the intellectual, to the psychic, then to the spiritual as one proceeds from faith alone, to faith and experiences that are obtained through experimentation.

But a major problem persists. How can one say something spiritual to another without upsetting that individual's innermost sensitivities especially when that person is not ready to receive this information and the latter infringes on their comfort zone?

Some persons adamantly refuse to even listen to this information. It is their right of course. As stated earlier, individual sensitivities can be extremely heightened when sharing new information on God's kingdoms. Therefore, the person sharing this information must know when to say a little, or when to say much, when to rapidly change the subject, or when to be silent.

In seeking God, one has to realize that one must transition from a child of God, to an adult of God as soon as possible. But one of the most difficult challenges is to plant a seed of new information in the sciences or the arts. Furthermore, it is even more difficult when the subject matter relates to the psychic, and spirituality, and has not been heard before.

Many persons either pattern their lives after some perceived model that reflects their views, those of family or friends, or a combination of the two. Is is incumbent, however, that the model reflects complete and up-to-date information in a continuing evolving world.

As one proceeds from the intellectual, to the psychic, and then to the spiritual, one observes increasingly that one appears to tap in to the harmony of life itself.

For examples, when driving, one might run out of gas a few feet from a gas station: in a crowded shopping mall, a lone parking spot can beckon; or a highway sign might warn to "buckle up or ticket," when one's seatbelt were unbuckled. These incidents are examples of waking dreams (see Klemp – (6).

Also needed is faith in what one is pursuing, competent guidance, dedication to the work, perseverence, trust, optimism, enthusiasm, anticipation of successful outcomes, motivation, resilience, as well as requisite experiences that can be obtained from experimentation. All of the above prepare the reader for a better chance of being ready to appreciate any new information on God.

In one's quest for awareness, three other points should be made. First, from recent information, although immature, Soul wants to survive in order to secure the experiences while in the body that are needed for its development. However, the mind often involves the body in activities that are detrimental to this structure. Soul then tries to intercede but can be overruled. The result can be premature death of the body, and unfortunately, termination of Soul's training in this incarnation.

Furthermore, once one knows that one is Soul, is one willing to undergo the multifaceted challenges that lie ahead?

Second, for each pathway, as one goes horizontally (that is, from the elementary, to the intermediate, and then to the advanced), and vertically (also from the elementary, to the intermediate, and then to the advanced), one observes generally that individual activity replaces group activity.

Third, some consider activities such as seeking an education, and then employment, raising a family, and pursuing some type of career as self-sponsored, whereas choosing a path in old-age and modern religions, or other psychic pathways, as God-sponsored. However, if all the activities listed above as self-sponsored were considered as God-sponsored, then there may be less reluctance to seek greater experiences about God by means of experimentation.

The path called old-age and modern religions is very dear to the hearts of many individuals. Others do not even want to discuss the subject – a sacred cow, literally. But if treated as any other subject of inquiry, such as economics, scientific thinking, or history, then many truths about God can now be revealed especially if the fear factor is eliminated.

Therefore, the term religion today does not adequately describe God and His works. Also needed are terms such as Physics, Biology, Mathematics, Economics, Chemistry, Mysticism, and Spirituality, to name a few.

On the other hand, the path called Spirituality faces many challenges. First, it has to debunk the many myths regarding God and His kingdoms. Second, it has to provide current information in an evolving world that leads to a viable pathway to God, which it does.

Third, it has to endeavor to raise the consciousness of mankind when asleep, among other things, from zero percent or a little beyond zero percent, to as close to 100 percent as possible, fully realizing that when the 100 percent mark is reached, the consciousness bar will have been raised to a much higher level. The reason is that in spiritual development, there is always one more step to take.

When working for God as a Co-worker, His expectations are not what most persons believe them to be. Respect replaces worship; bravery as an eagle substitutes for timidity as a dove, and eagerness to assist in His creations becomes extremely important. One should also expect to shoulder greater responsibilities, and to convert liabilities into assets, and weaknesses into strengths.

In the quest for awareness, one must also analyze one's efficiency, on a daily or regular basis, in completing tasks that one has set for one's self. What percentage of tasks planned is actually completed?

In addition, interesting questions for the reader to answer can be, "What percentage of God's kingdoms is examined by the pathways or sub-pathways that follow:- a. The Intellectual pathway? b. The Psychic pathway – Old Age and Modern Religions? c. The Psychic pathway – Mysticism? and d. The Spiritual pathway – Eckankar or Advanced Religion?"

It appears that information about God does not present itself as a single package of knowledge but as multiple bits of data, of increasing complexity, that fit, a particular level of consciousness.

Finally, information about God has been presented at three different levels. It is now up to the reader to decide whether or not to explore this information further, and if so, at what level. Based on the pathway that one may have pursued in the past, is currently pursuing, or intends to pursue, is one's present pursuit of a pathway to God intermediate intellectual, elementary psychic, elementary spiritual, or another? One has a lot of territory to cover in aspiring to God awareness in this lifetime. Most important of all, one has to endeavor to stay the course that one has charted for one's self. The information presented can be considered the missing link in our spiritual evolution.

Literature Cited

1. Twitchell, Paul. *The Tiger's Fang*. Eckankar, Minneapolis, MN., 1967.

2. ----------------- *The Shariyat-Ki-Sugmad,* Book 1. Eckankar, Minneapolis, MN., 1970.

3. -----------------. Eckankar, *The Key to Secret Worlds*. Eckankar, Minneapolis, MN., 1969.

4. Klemp, Harold. *We Come as Eagles*. Mahanta Transcripts, Book 9., Eckankar, Minneapolis, MN., 1994.

5. -----------------. *The Dream Master*. Mahanta Transcripts, Book 8, Eckankar, Minneapolis, MN., 1993.

6. -----------------. *The Secret of Love*. Mahanta Transcripts, Book 14. Eckankar, Minneapolis, MN., 1996.

7. Solomon, Eldra P. and P. William Davis. *Human Anatomy and Physiology*. Saunders College Publishing, Philadelphia, PA., 1983.

8. Gardner, Eldon J. and D. Peter Snustad. *Principles of Genetics*, 6th ed. John Wiley and Sons, New York, NY., 1981.

9. Twitchell, Paul. *The Shariyat-Ki-Sugmad*, Book 2. Eckankar, Minneapolis, MN., 1971.

10. Klemp, Harold. *Journey of Soul*, 2nd ed. Mahanta Transcripts Book 1. Eckankar, Minneapolis, MN., 1988.

11. Twitchell, Paul. *The Spiritual Notebook*. Eckankar, Minneapolis, MN., 1971.

12. Klemp, Harold. *Those Wonderful ECK Masters*. Eckankar, Minneapolis, MN., 2005.

13. Leadbeater, Charles W. *The Chakras*. Theosophical Publishing House, Wheaton, IL., 1972.

14. Motoyama, Hiroshi. *Theories of the Chakras: Bridge to Higher Consciousness*. Theosophical Publishing House, Wheaton, IL., 1981.

15. Willson, Terrill. *How I Learned Soul Travel*. Eckankar, Minneapolis, MN., 1987.

16. Klemp, Harold. *How to Find God*. Mahanta Transcripts, Book 2. Eckankar, Minneapolis, MN., 1988.

17. Twitchell, Paul. *The ECK-Vidya: Ancient Science of Prophecy*. Eckankar, Minneapolis, MN., 1972.

18. Klemp, Harold. *The Book of ECK Parables*, Vol. 1. Eckankar, Minneapolis, MN., 1986.

19. ------------------. *A Cosmic Sea of Words: The Eckankar Lexicon*. Eckankar, Minneapolis, MN., 1998.

20. Leslie-Smith, H. (ed.). *The Esoteric Writings of Helena Petrovna Blavatsky*. Theosophical Publishling House, Wheaton, IL., 1980.

21. Lewis, H, Spencer. *The Mystical Life of Jesus*. Supreme Grand Lodge of AMORC, San Jose, CA, 1973.

22. Cihlar, Many. *Mystics at Prayer.* Supreme Grand Lodge of AMORC, San Jose, CA., 1974.

23. Lewis, H, Spencer. *Mansions of the Soul: The Cosmic Conception.* Supreme Grand Lodge of AMORC, San Jose, CA., 1975.

24. Lewis, Ralph M. Martinist Documents: Traditional Martinist Order, Rosicrucian Press, San Jose, Ca., 1977.

25. Rose, C. R. *Fundamental Approaches in Mastering the Sciences: A Comprehensive Guide for Students.* C. H. Fairfax Co., Publishers, Baltimore, MD., 1991.

26. Verkade, P. E. "August Kekule." *Proceedings of the Chemical Society*, 204, 1958.

27. Walker Jr., Warren F. *Vertebrate Dissection*, 4th ed. W. B. Saunders Co., Philadelphia, PA., 1970.

28. Moore, Keith L. *The Developing Human: Clinically Oriented Embryology*, 4th ed. W. B. Saunders Co., Philadephia, PA., 1988.

29. Barrett, David B., George T. Kurian, and Todd M. Johnson. *World Christian Encyclopedia: A Comprehensive Survey of Church and Religions in the Modern World.* Vol. 2: The World by Segments-Religions, Peoples, Languages, Cities, Topics, 2nd ed. Oxford University Press, New York, NY., 2001.

30. Adherents.com.html. Major Religions of the World Ranked by Number of Adherents. Adherents.com.html, 2005.

31. Devinne, Pamela B. (ed.). *The American Heritage Dictionary,* 2nd ed., Houghton Mifflin Co., Boston, MA, 1985.

32. Ozaniec, Naomi. *The Elements of the Chakras.* Element Books, Longmeads, Shaftesbury, Dorset, England, England, 1990.

33. Collins, William. *The Holy Bible.* Collins Clear-Type Press, London, England, 1959.

34. Klemp, Harold. *The Slow Burning Love of God.* Mahanta Transcripts, Book 13. Eckankar, Minneapolis, MN., 1997.

35. -------------------. *Past Lives, Dreams, and Soul Travel.* Eckankar. Minneapolis, MN., 2003.

36. Eckankar. *The Worlds of ECK Chart.* Eckankar (www.Eckankar. org/Image/godworlds.pdf), Minneapolis, MN, 2002.

Index

D

Daily karma 14. *See* Karma types
Death xi, 1–3, 6, 7, 9, 14, 33, 37, 44, 51
Devil, the xiii, 9, 12, 13, 19, 29, 41
Duality 12, 27

E

ECK 9, 13, 41
Eckankar xii, 5, 10, 13, 15, 17, 18, 20, 21, 29, 30, 39, 41, 44, 49, 52. *See* Chapter 8
    comprehensive dream analysis 43
    Shariyat-Ki-Sugmad 44
    The Living Master 12, 43
Emotions 12
Energies 21, 38
    energy channels 38. *See* Chakras
    prana 38
    vital energy 38
    vital life force 38
Essenes 37
Evolution 2, 19, 26, 37, 49, 52
    human kidney 27
    jaw structures 27
Exercise 24, 35, 38, 44, 45
Experimentation xii, 25, 30, 31, 35–37, 44, 49–51

F

Faith xii, 30, 35, 36, 43, 50
Fate karma 14. *See* karma types
Fear 12, 42–44, 51
    of death 44
Former lives 12

G

Gnostics 37

God xi–xiii, 1–13, 15, 17–19, 20, 21, 23–25, 27, 29–31, 33–37, 39, 41–45, 47–52

Grandparents 8
Greed xiii, 9, 12, 14, 43. *See* Mind passions

H

Headquarters of 34
    Eckankar 41, 44
    old-age and modern religions 34
Heart 38, 44, 51. *See* Chakras
Heavens (Planes) of God 44
    Access to the planes of God 11
    psychic planes 11, 42
    spiritual planes 11, 42, 44
Holy Spirit 19, 31, 39, 42, 43
Homing beacons for Soul 13, 42
HU 33, 45
Human body xi, 7, 9, 24, 33
Humans 2, 3, 23, 26, 27
Hypothesis 25, 45, 49
    access to God's kingdoms is from within, and not from without 45

I

Illness 1, 15, 38, 39
Immature Soul 42. *See* Soul
Inner nudges 4
Intellectual xi, xiii, 1–4, 6–10, 13, 17, 19–21, 23, 24, 25, 27, 29, 33, 45, 47, 49, 50
Intellectual pathway 3, 7, 9, 13, 17, 19, 21, 23, 25, 27, 29, 34–36, 38, 44, 47, 52
Intellectual training 7, 13, 24, 25

J

Jehovah 6, 9, 11, 31
Jesus 9, 31, 33, 37, 45
　　second coming 6, 33

K

Karma xii, 11, 13–15, 39, 44
　　types of karma 14
　　　　Adi Karma 13, 14
　　　　Daily Karma 14
　　　　Fate Karma 14
　　　　Reserve Karma 14
Karmaless action 14, 15
Kekule, August xii, 26
Klemp, Sri Harold 43. See Living ECK
　　Master (Teacher); See Mahanta;
　　See Wayshower
Krisna 31

L

Levitation 39. See Resurrection
Life xi, xiii, 1–6, 9, 14, 26, 33, 34, 38,
　　39, 49
　　loving of all 4
Lifetimes 4, 15, 25, 43
　　need for multiple lifetimes 25
Light 12, 13, 27, 31, 37, 42, 43
Living ECK Master (Teacher) 9, 13, 41.
　　See Wayshower; See Mahanta
　　Godman 42
Living things 23
　　living things are Soul 23
Lords of Karma 13
Love 12, 14, 44
　　divine love 44
Lust xiii, 9, 12, 14, 43. See Mind
　　passions

M

Mahanta. See Living ECK Master
　　(Teacher)
Meditation 27, 36, 37, 49
Meridians 37–38
Mind xii, xiii, 4, 7, 9, 12–14, 19, 23,
　　24, 26, 27, 35, 42–44, 47, 51.
　　See Soul/physical body part (p.
　　42)
Mind passions xiii. See Anger; See Greed;
　　See Lust; See Vanity
　　attachment to material possessions
　　　　xiii, 9, 12, 14, 43
Mohammed 31, 45
Motoyama, Hiroshi 38, 39
Mystery schools 36
Mysticism xi, 6, 17, 19–21, 29, 30, 33–
　　35, 36–38, 42, 43, 51, 52

N

Nadis 37, 38
New-age religion 17, 41. See Advanced
　　religion, Spirituality, or
　　Eckankar
Nobel laureate 27, 44

O

Objective xi, xii, 6, 19, 23, 25, 26, 33.
　　See Techniques; See Scientific
　　Method; See Intellectual
　　pathway
　　objective consciousness xii
　　objective method 23, 25
　　objective senses 19
　　objective techniques 23
Old-age and modern religions xi, xii, 4,
　　6, 7, 17, 19, 20, 29, 30, 33, 34–36,
　　41, 42, 49, 51
Other living things 23
　　other living things are Soul 23

P

Parents and Grandparents 8
Particle of God 23
Passions of the mind 9, 12, 14, 43.
    See Mind passions
Past lives 2, 43
    plane 3 12
Planes of God 11, 44
Prayer 30, 33, 36
Psychic xiii, 2, 3, 6–8, 10, 17, 20, 21,
    25–27, 29, 39, 47, 49, 50, 52.
    See Subjective Techniques
    healing 39
    training 7
Puppet 4

R

Reincarnation xii, 14, 15, 25, 26, 44
Religion xi, xii, xiii, 4–7, 10, 13, 15, 17,
    19, 20, 29–31, 32–36, 39, 41–43,
    49, 51, 52
Reserve karma 14. See types of Karma
Residence of Soul on earth xi, 7
Resurrection 6, 33
    is not of the physical body 6
    is of the spiritual self 33
Rosicrucians 37

S

Scientific method 25, 26, 33, 35, 44
Senses xi, xii, 7, 19, 23–26, 30, 35
Society of the Golden Dawn 20, 37
Soul xi, xii, 2, 4, 6, 7, 13–15, 19, 23, 24,
    31, 33, 35, 38, 42, 44, 47, 51
Soul travel xii, 9, 34, 44
Sound 7, 12, 13, 31, 37, 38, 42, 43
    sound of a flute 12, 13
    sound of thunder 12, 13
Spiritual development xiii, 2–4, 42, 52

Spirituality xii, 2, 5, 13, 17, 18, 29,
    30, 33, 34, 36, 39, 41, 42–45,
    49–51. See advanced religion;
    See Eckankar
Spirituality (Advanced Religion)
    contemplation 12, 13, 27, 36, 37,
    43, 44
Spiritual Masters 9, 13, 27, 34, 35,
    43. See Living ECK Master
    (Teacher)
Spiritual pathway xii, 4, 6, 9, 10, 13, 19,
    21, 41, 44, 47, 52
Spiritual pathway (Spirituality).
    See Advanced religion;
    See Eckankar; See Pathways into
    God's Kingdoms
Spiritual training 7, 10
Subjective xii, 6, 7, 19, 23, 25, 26, 29,
    30, 35, 38, 44
    subjective method 26
    subjective senses 26
    subjective techniques xii, 23, 29
Systems, bodily 7, 24
    Circulatory 7
    Digestive 7
    Excretory 7
    Genetic 7
    Immune 7
    Integumentary 7
    Lymphatic 7
    Nervous 7
    Reproductive 7
    Respiratory 7
    Skeletal 7
    Urinary 7

T

Teachers xiii, 13, 38
Techniques xii, 12, 23, 25–27, 29, 30,
    34, 38, 39, 43
The Theosophical Society 37

Selected Pathways

to

God

Colliston R. Rose, MD

Free Preview

From a recent review of the literature, it is clear that seeking an education, then employment, raising a family if desired and pursuing rest and relaxation are all secondary to working with the Creator as a Co-worker in an increasingly responsible manner.

For many persons, life begins in the cradle and ends at the grave. However, evidence is mounting that one survives death not in the physical form but in the spiritual. We are Soul, a spark of God. Soul is immortal. Furthermore, for us, the human body is the temporary residence of Soul while on earth, and from which it departs and returns during sleep, or leaves permanently at death. Soul's quest is to be a Co-worker with God and eventually, to return to its kingdoms, its true home.

God lives on floor twelve of a spiritual mansion, literally; by comparison the earth is floor one. Therefore, Soul seeks a two-, or three-pronged education on earth, and elsewhere, to find a job, pay a rent, raise a family if desired, and find ways to return to its true home. In so doing, it must convert its immaturity to maturity, and spiritual infancy to mastership.

Two well-known training pathways exist for taking Soul into God's kingdoms while still living. These are the Intellectual, favored by science and others, that uses the five physical, or objective, senses and the Psychic (such as old-age and modern religions, yoga, Mysticism, and others), that employs the five spiritual, or subjective senses.

Since 1965, however, a third major pathway that existed since time immemorial but which was either hidden, or cryptic, emerged. This is Advanced religion (Eckankar) or Spirituality, that also employs the subjective senses. These three pathways can be rank-ordered and relate to how far into God's kingdoms one can reach.

It may be a surprise to learn that each of us has three educational paths to pursue, if not already pursued. As said earlier, these are the Intellectual, or objective, that can take one one-sixth of the way into God's kingdoms: the Psychic, or subjective, that prepares one for almost half of the journey; and the Spiritual, also subjective, that has the potential to reach all the way into God's kingdoms.

Training in intellectualism, psychic matters, as well as spirituality, in that order, takes one to increasingly higher levels of understanding and experiences, from fringe to full, that an individual not receiving this training may not believe or even consider possible until this person has received a similar level of instruction.

The Intellectual pathway largely prepares one for life on earth; whereas, the Psychic and Spiritual pathways largely prepare one for life after death of the physical body, although these can be pursued while one is still alive.

Furthermore, each of these pathways has three different sub-levels, namely, the elementary, the intermediate, and the advanced. This meant that before 1965, those persons choosing a pathway to God, or had one chosen for them, involved themselves lacking all of the information on pathways that is available today.

Although it is one's right to choose a pathway to God that fulfils one's needs, this should be done after all possible information on pathways is examined, not before.

The text introduces the pathways mentioned, use of two very distinct mechanisms (the mind and Soul) for gleaning information about God, karma and reincarnation that allow one to visit past mistakes for corrective action, as well as the vital need to convert faith and belief into knowledge by means of experimentation.

In old-age and modern religions for the congregation, for example, there is very little, if any, experimentation beyond singing, dancing, prayer, feasting, and fasting, and even these are not structured for the collection and analysis of data. In trance-like experiments, the experimentee is not conscious of what transpires.

Other psychic pathways and the Spiritual pathway, on the other hand, feature profound experimentation for new and advanced students.

Experimentation increases one's awareness (consciousness) considerably while awake as well as when asleep. Experimentation can enhance the development of subjective techniques such as chakra awakening, intuition, exteriorization of consciousness, dream travel, Soul travel, and so on.

Additional discussion examines the mind passions that can preclude spiritual development. These are represented by the acronym, vagal – vanity, anger, greed, attachment to material possessions, and lust. This story of life itself features a Living Master and the devil as teachers and educators.

But a major problem persists. How can one say something spiritual to another without upsetting that individual's innermost sensitivities especially when that person is not ready to receive this information and the latter infringes on their comfort zone? Some persons adamantly refuse to even listen to this information.

In seeking God, one has to realize that one must transition from a child of God, to an adult of God as soon as possible.

When working for God as a Co-worker, His expectations are not what most persons believe them to be. Respect replaces worship; bravery as an eagle substitutes for timidity as a dove, and eagerness to assist in His creations becomes extremely important. One should also expect to shoulder greater responsibilities, and to convert liabilities into assets, and weaknesses into strengths.

In addition, interesting questions for the reader to answer can be, "What percentage of God's kingdoms is examined by the pathways or sub-pathways that follow:- a. The Intellectual pathway? b. The Psychic pathway – Old age and modern religions? c. The Psychic pathway – Mysticism? and, d. The Spiritual pathway – Eckankar or Advanced Religion?"

The focus of this book is an elementary understanding of God and His kingdoms that is not fully detail-oriented. The reader will have to consult with the various appropriate organizations and programs that can provide this information, whether they be the intellectual, the psychic, or the spiritual.

Finally, information about God has been presented at three different levels. It is now up to the reader to decide whether or not to explore this information further, and if so, at what level.